I0475794

I. Introduction

Hospital mergers can lead to higher prices and lower quality for consumers by reducing competition. Hospital mergers can also enable hospitals to achieve scale and scope economies that may ultimately benefit consumers. Balancing these two opposing effects involves identifying the set of hospitals that currently or soon will compete with the merging hospitals, predicting the post-merger behavior of the merging hospitals and their competitors, and assessing whether scale and scope economies likely outweigh the harm from any possible loss of competition. This paper considers one question that relates to the second issue: Do nonprofit hospitals, which are barred from paying out any surplus as profit, exercise market power? If nonprofit hospitals exercise market power, then antitrust enforcement should challenge hospital mergers that create market power without creating offsetting efficiency benefits. However, if nonprofit hospitals choose not to exercise market power, then antitrust enforcement of hospital mergers should be restricted to those markets in which a nonprofit hospital can not offset anticompetitive behavior by for-profit hospitals.

Several theories seek to explain the behavior of nonprofit hospitals. While all of these theories assume that some constituency controls the nonprofit hospital and uses this control to pursue some objective, the theories differ in the identity of the controlling constituency and the objective pursued. One theory argues that independent, nonprofit hospitals behave as consumer cooperatives.[1] According to this theory, community representation on a nonprofit hospital's board of directors ensures that the nonprofit hospital will set competitive prices even when the nonprofit hospital possesses market power.[2]

---

[1] See Lynk (1994).

[2] Several recent court cases have considered this argument. While the court accepted this argument in U.S. v. Carilion Health System, 707 F.Supp. 840 (W.D. Vir. 1989) and FTC v. Butterworth Health Corp. and Blodgett Memorial Medical Center, No. 1:96-CV-49 (W.D.MI Sept. 26, 1996), the court rejected this argument in U.S. v. Rockford Memorial Corporation, 717 F.Supp. 1251 (N.D.Ill. 1989), aff'd, 898 F.2d 1278 (7th Cir. 1990).

Several other theories assume that hospital administrators control nonprofit hospitals. The first of these theories assumes that hospital administrators seek to maximize the hospital's output. Thus, this theory predicts that a nonprofit hospital would not exercise market power since doing so would only reduce the number of patients served. The second of these theories assumes that hospital administrators obtain utility from both the quantity and the quality of a hospital's output.[3] The desire to increase the quality of the output may prompt a hospital to offer a higher quality of service than consumers want. Thus, in this theory, nonprofit hospitals may exploit market power in order to subsidize services that are not economically viable. The third of these theories assumes that hospital administrators seek to provide care for indigent patients. This theory predicts that nonprofit hospitals would exercise market power against privately insured patients in order to provide more indigent care. The fourth of these theories assumes that hospital administrators seek perquisites such as fancier offices or an easy life. In this theory, nonprofit hospitals might exploit market power in order to have a larger surplus that can support more perquisites or inefficient operations.

One final theory argues that nonprofit hospitals are controlled by their medical staffs.[4] In this theory, whether the hospital exploits market power depends on the hospital's policy toward granting staff privileges. If physicians can freely enter and obtain staff privileges, then both hospital care and physician care will be provided competitively: A hospital's medical staff generally has an interest in keeping prices low because an increase in the price of hospital care in an area reduces the demand for physician services in that area. Suppose, however, that the hospital's existing medical staff can limit entry but cannot restrict the profits of those physicians that they allow to enter. In this case, entry by new physicians dilutes the monopoly rents that incumbent staff physicians can obtain. Consequently, staff physicians have an incentive to meet increased demand by using more hospital care (e.g., excess

---

[3] See Newhouse (1970).

[4] See Pauly and Redisch (1973).

2

bed capacity) rather than increasing the number of staff physicians. This increases the cost of hospital care. Where this occurs, medical care is both monopolized and produced inefficiently by combining too little physician services and too much hospital services.

Several of the theories described above predict that nonprofit hospitals do not exploit market power, while several of the theories predict that they do. This paper examines the behavior of hospitals in California in order to differentiate between these two possibilities. Section II of the paper reviews previous empirical studies, Section III describes the model and the data, Section IV presents the results, and Section V concludes.

II. Literature Review

Two previous studies consider how nonprofit hospitals behave when they have market power.[5] Lynk (1995) tests whether the relationship between price and market power differs for nonprofit, for-profit, and government hospitals. Lynk measures market power as a hospital's share of admissions in the county where it is located and as the Herfindahl-Hirschman Index for that county. Although Lynk estimates several specifications, let us focus on two in which the dependent variable is a hospital's price. In the first, Lynk uses slope dummy variables to test whether the relationship between price and market share differs for nonprofit, for-profit, and government hospitals. Using this specification, Lynk finds a positive relationship for for-profit hospitals and a negative relationship for nonprofit and government hospitals. However, none of these relationships is statistically significant.

In the second specification, Lynk uses two variables, market share and HHI, to measure market power. He then uses slope dummy variables to test whether the relationships between net price and market share and net price and HHI differ for nonprofit, for-profit, and government hospitals.

---

[5] A number of empirical studies examine generally whether nonprofit hospitals behave differently than for-profit hospitals. These include Watt et al. (1986), Sloan and Vraciu (1983), Hoerger (1991), and Norton and Staiger (1994).

For each ownership type, the sign of the coefficient for market share differs from the sign of the coefficient for HHI. This prevents any simple interpretation of these coefficients. However, Lynk does use these coefficients and the mean values for market share to simulate the effect of a merger of two hospitals of the same ownership class. Lynk estimates that a merger of two for-profit hospitals would increase net price by 8.7 percent, a merger between two government hospitals would increase price by 2.5 percent, and a merger between two nonprofit hospitals would decrease price by 4.1 percent. The results for the nonprofit and government hospitals are statistically significant at the 5 percent level, while the result for the for-profit hospitals falls just short of being statistically significant at the 10 percent level. Thus, Lynk's results suggest that nonprofit hospitals do not exploit market power, for-profit hospitals do exploit market power, and government hospitals exploit market power to a small extent.

Lynk's results, while interesting, should probably be viewed with some caution. Melnick et al. (1992) and Dranove et al. (1993) find a positive relationship between price and concentration in samples that include nonprofit, for-profit, and government hospitals in California. Melnick et al., for instance, calculate that moving from an HHI of 3333 to 5000 would lead to a price increase of 9 percent. Lynk's results are consistent with these studies only if the positive relationships between price and market power that he finds for for-profit and government hospitals dominate the negative relationship between price and market power that he finds for nonprofit hospitals. This seems unlikely given the magnitude of these relationships and the composition of his sample. Of the hospitals in his sample, 20 percent are for-profit, 28 percent are government, and 52 percent are nonprofit.

In the second study, Gruber (1994) examines the effect of increased price shopping over the 1984-1988 period on the provision of uncompensated care by California hospitals. Gruber finds that net income for nonprofit hospitals rose more slowly in less concentrated markets than in more concentrated markets. He also finds that the amount of uncompensated care provided by nonprofit

4

hospitals in less concentrated markets fell relative to the amount provided by nonprofit hospitals in more concentrated markets.[6] From these two results, Gruber concludes that nonprofit hospitals in less concentrated markets provided less uncompensated care over the 1984-1988 period because increased price competition decreased the market power, and thus the net income, of these hospitals.[7] Thus, Gruber's results suggest that nonprofit hospitals exploit market power and use part of the surplus to fund indigent care.

III. Model, Variable Descriptions, and Data

A. Model

We model a hospital's pricing behavior as:[8]

$$P_i = f(MC_i, E_i O_i)$$
$$E_i = g(M, L_i, \lambda_i)$$

That is, the price that a hospital charges (P_i) should reflect its marginal cost of providing care (MC_i) and the elasticity of demand that it faces (E_i) interacted with its objective function (O_i). In turn, the hospital specific elasticity of demand (E_i) depends on the market elasticity of demand (M), the location of other hospitals (L_i), and the competitive behavior of these hospitals (λ_i).

To capture these various effects, we estimate the following reduced form model in which the variables enter linearly.[9] The variables are described below.

---

[6] See Gruber (1994), p. 204.

[7] Gruber estimates that a 1 percent decline in hospital resources led to between a 0.4 and 1 percent decline in uncompensated care.

[8] This basically follows McDonald (1987).

[9] We also estimate a double log-linear model. The signs and statistical significance of the

(continued...)

$$PRICE = \alpha_1 + \alpha_2 PROFIT + \beta_1 MARKETPOWER + \beta_2 PROFIT*MARKETPOWER$$

$$+ \beta_3 CASEMIX + \beta_4 ALOS + \beta_5 LONGTERM + \beta_6 WAGEINDEX$$

$$+ \beta_7 INCOME + \beta_8 BEDSIZE + \epsilon$$

B. Variable Descriptions

Price

PRICE is the average price paid per inpatient, acute-care admission for privately insured patients. PRICE is computed by multiplying the total net revenues from privately insured patients by the ratio of gross *inpatient* revenue from privately insured patients over the gross *total* revenue from privately insured patients. This yields an estimate of the net *inpatient* revenue from privately insured patients.[10] The price paid per admission for privately insured patients is this amount divided by the total number of discharges of privately insured patients.[11]

Market Power

_____

(...continued)
variables generally do not change. (See Models 5 and 6 in Appendix A).

[10] A hospital's net revenue equals its gross revenue minus any discounts that it offers. Since hospitals generally offer substantial discounts, computing PRICE using net revenue rather than gross revenue is preferable.

[11] The data that we use groups indigent patients and privately insured patients into a category called "other third party." We adjust the number of "other third party" discharges by the ratio (total revenue - bad debt)/total revenue. This yields an estimate of the number of discharges of privately insured patients. Dividing net inpatient revenue from privately insured patients by this estimate yields PRICE.

Factors affecting a hospital's market power include the distance to surrounding hospitals, the size and service mix of these hospitals, and the behavior of these hospitals. Because no single measure of market power can fully capture all of these factors, we use two alternative measures of market power. Each has advantages and disadvantages.

HHI, our first measure of market power, computes a Herfindahl-Hirschman Index based on the licensed beds of the acute-care hospitals within a county. While HHI accounts for the presence and relative size of the acute-care hospitals within the defined market, HHI has several disadvantages. First, the definition of the market is arbitrary.[12] Second, HHI accounts for neither localized competition within the market nor competition outside of the market. For instance, an HHI of 10,000 does not necessarily indicate whether a hospital's closest competitor is five miles away or fifty miles away. Third, HHI imperfectly measures market power if hospitals exploit market power differentially based on their ownership: A hospital that shares a market with a for-profit hospital may have more market power than a hospital that shares a market with a nonprofit hospital.[13]

---

[12]   In previous studies of hospital pricing behavior, Noether (1988) defined markets as metropolitan statistical areas, Staten et al. (1988) and Lynk (1995) defined markets as counties, and Dranove et al. (1993) defined markets as urbanized areas. These definitions are also arbitrary. Melnick et al. (1992) defined markets based on actual patient flow. We were reluctant to do this because of possible endogeneity problems.
    We also computed HHI by defining geographic markets as a 15-mile radius around an urban hospital and a 20-mile radius around a rural hospital. The estimated coefficient for HHI changes little when we define markets this way.

[13] If nonprofit hospitals behave as fringe competitors irrespective of their market share, then presumably the square of their market shares should not be included in computing HHI. (e.g., if a for-profit and a nonprofit hospital each had a 50 percent market share, then the HHI should be 2500 not 5000.) We regressed PRICE on the HHI computed using all hospitals, the HHI computed using only for-profit hospitals, and the control variables described later. We found that the HHI computed using all hospitals is statistically significant while the HHI computed using only for-profits is not. This suggests that the HHI computed for all hospitals is the better measure of market power

MINDIST1, the second measure of market power, measures market power as the distance from a hospital to its next closest competitor.[14] A hospital's ability to charge a higher price depends on the consumer surplus enjoyed by its marginal consumers. This consumer surplus depends on the cost to these consumers of switching to more distant hospitals. Much of this cost is the travel cost required to obtain care at more distant hospitals. MINDIST1 proxies for this travel cost. Like HHI, MINDIST1 may measure market power with error. First, the distance to a hospital's other competitors may affect a hospital's market power. Second, the relative size of a hospital's competitors may affect a consumer's willingness to switch to these competitors. Third, the pricing behavior of a hospital's competitors may affect a hospital's market power. This pricing behavior may be affected by the competitor's ownership and by the competitive situation faced by the competitor.

Both HHI and MINDIST1 may be endogenous. For example, by charging a high price, a hospital decreases the likelihood that a neighboring hospital will exit and increases the likelihood that an entrant will locate nearby. While the reader should be cautious of possible endogeneity bias in interpreting both our results and the results of other price-concentration studies (including Lynk (1995)), for two reasons, we believe that endogeneity bias in our study is less serious than in price-concentration studies of some other industries. First, Medicare demand accounts for roughly 40 percent of inpatient hospital days. Hospitals have limited discretion to exploit market power toward Medicare patients because Medicare pays hospitals a fixed rate. Second, to a large extent, the location and licensed beds of hospitals is determined by previously-made decisions. Many of these decisions were made in an environment substantially different than the environment in 1993. Prior to 1983, price competition among hospitals was attenuated because California did not allow insurers to contract

---

[14] We assigned each hospital in the data set the latitude and longitude coordinates of the post office in their zip code. $DISTANCE_j$ is the distance between hospital$_i$'s coordinates and hospital$_j$'s coordinates. MINDIST is the smallest DISTANCE for which hospital$_j$ has at least 40 percent of the licensed beds as hospital$_i$. (We also measured MINDIST as the smallest DISTANCE for which hospital$_j$ has at least 25 percent of the licensed beds as hospital$_i$. The results changed little.)

8

selectively with hospitals (Gruber (1994)). Prior to 1987, California's CON regulation affected both hospital entry and hospital size.

Ownership

The data we use classifies hospitals into four categories based on ownership: nonprofit, for-profit, government, and district. For-profit, government, and district hospitals should not be included in our sample if they behave differently than nonprofit hospitals with respect to the other control variables, which are described later. To test whether this is the case, we interact dummy variables for for-profit, government, and district hospitals with the market power control variables and with the other control variables. We then estimate our model using these interaction terms. With respect to the other control variables, an F-test for each set of interaction terms indicates whether an ownership class (e.g., for-profit hospitals) behaves the same as nonprofit hospitals. With respect to the other control variables, these F-tests indicate that we can reject the hypothesis that government hospitals behave the same as nonprofit hospitals at the 1 percent level, but that we can not reject the hypothesis that for-profit and district hospitals behave the same as nonprofit hospitals at even the 10 percent level. Based on this, we include for-profit and district hospitals in our sample, but we delete government hospitals.

District hospitals are nonprofit hospitals that have a publicly elected board and can levy taxes. District hospitals tend to be smaller than other hospitals and tend to serve rural areas. Although Lynk (1995) treats district hospitals as government hospitals, we believe that district hospitals are more similar to nonprofit hospitals than to government hospitals. Consequently, we group district hospitals and nonprofit hospitals together into one nonprofit category. This leaves two ownership classes, nonprofit and for-profit, in our sample.

The intercept dummy variable PROFIT measures any difference in the intercepts for nonprofit and for-profit hospitals. Interacting

9

this dummy variable with MARKET POWER allows the relationship between PRICE and MARKET POWER to vary for nonprofit and for-profit hospitals while allowing the observations for both ownership classes to be used in computing the coefficients of the other control variables.[15] Given this specification, the coefficient for the MARKETPOWER variable (either HHI or MINDIST) measures the relationship between price and market power for nonprofit hospitals. The sum of the coefficient for the MARKET POWER variable (either HHI or MINDIST1) and the coefficient for the interaction term (either PROFIT*HHI or PROFIT*MINDIST1) measures the relationship between price and market power for for-profit hospitals.

Other Control Variables

Six variables control for the cost of care that a hospital provides. CASEMIX, which measures a hospital's case mix, should control for much of the difference in the complexity of care provided by different hospitals. CASEMIX is computed in the following manner for each of the hospitals in the sample. For all of the inpatient discharges in California, OSHPAD's patient discharge data set records the hospital at which the patient received care, the diagnosis related group (DRG) for which the patient received care, and the source of payment. For privately insured patients, each discharge was weighted using the Health Care Financing Administration's DRG weights. For each hospital, these weighted discharges were summed and then divided by the total number of discharges of privately insured patients from that hospital. CASEMIX may not fully account for differences in the complexity of care that hospitals provide because the severity of an illness differs even within DRG's. The coefficient for CASEMIX should be positive. ALOS is the average length of stay for a hospital's privately insured patients. ALOS represents a second measure of the quality of care provided by a hospital since

---

[15] We also regress PRICE on MARKETPOWER and the other control variables for a sample of only nonprofit and district hospitals. The results are presented in tables 8 and 9 in Appendix A.

hospitals with longer average lengths of stay are likely treating sicker patients. The coefficient for ALOS should be positive.[16] LONGTERM measures the ratio of long-term days to total inpatient days. Long-term care, which includes skilled nursing care, intermediate care, and sub-acute care, is less expensive per day than is acute care. Because of the way some hospitals report their data, our measure of price for some hospitals will include some long-term days. LONGTERM, which is included to account for this, should be negative.

WAGEINDEX attempts to account for differences in wage rates across geographic areas. The Health Care Financing Administration, which administers Medicare, computes a wage index for various urban areas (a county or a set of counties) and for a composite statewide rural area.[17] In most cases, WAGEINDEX is simply the Medicare Wage Index for the county in which a hospital is located. However, where a rural hospital is located in an urban county, the Medicare Wage Index for the composite rural area replaces the county Medicare Wage Index. These rural hospitals are hospitals that either OSHPAD coded as rural hospitals or that serve a small city (e.g., Indio, Wildomar) that is more than 25 miles distant from a much larger metropolitan area. The coefficient for WAGEINDEX should be positive. INCOME, which is the 1989 per capita income for the city where the hospital is located,[18] proxies for any costs associated with providing greater comfort to affluent patients. For instance, affluent patients presumably would be more likely to demand private rooms. The coefficient for

---

[16] CASEMIX and ALOS are determined by three factors: The health of the population that the hospital treats, the relative cost of treating different illnesses (measured by the DRG weights), and a hospital's ability to provide advanced care. We believe that the first two factors are largely beyond a hospital's control. While a hospital does decide whether it will provide advanced care, we believe that this factor is largely determined by previous competitive conditions.

[17] Federal Register, Vol 60, No. 170, September 1, 1995, p 45883.

[18] For Los Angeles, which is a very large city in both area and population, we measure income as 1989 per capita income for the zip code where the hospital is located.

INCOME should be positive. Finally, BEDSIZE measures the number of licensed beds. The coefficient for BEDSIZE would be negative if scale economies enable large hospitals to produce inpatient acute care at lower cost than small hospitals. The coefficient for BEDSIZE would be positive if larger hospitals offer higher quality, higher cost care that is not picked up by our other control variables.[19]

C. Data Description and Sources

An observation is the price charged in 1993 by a general acute care hospital in California. Therefore, the data set excludes psychiatric hospitals, rehabilitation hospitals, specialty hospitals, and hospitals with a heavy nursing focus.[20] While all of the remaining hospitals are used in the computation of the HHI and MINDIST1 variables, ninety-two additional hospitals are excluded as observations. Thirty-six hospitals did not report sufficient data to compute PRICE.[21] Ten university teaching hospitals are deleted as observations because both their mission, which is to train physicians, and the type of care that they provide differ significantly from other hospitals.[22] Twenty-six hospitals are deleted from the sample because they had fewer than 100 discharges of private-pay patients in 1993 or because they had fewer than 20 staffed beds. Sixteen government hospitals are deleted for the

---

[19] While BEDSIZE may be endogenous, we believe that endogeneity bias is not serious for the reasons listed on page 8.

[20] OSHPAD groups hospitals into peer groups, which indicate the type of care that the hospital provides. The data set excludes hospitals in peer groups 1, 7-13, and 15-24. The data set also excludes five hospitals where the ratio of long-term days to total days exceeded 0.75 and several hospitals that the 1993 American Hospital Association does not categorize as general acute care hospitals. Finally, the data set excludes hospitals operated by Vencor, a chain of specialty hospitals, and THC Orange Hospital, which only had discharges in 9 DRG's in 1993.

[21] Twenty-five of these hospitals are operated by pre-paid health care plans such as Kaiser.

[22] OSHPAD coded nine of these hospitals as university teaching hospitals. We added USC-University Hospital to this list.

reasons discussed earlier. Two hospitals are deleted from the sample because they had a negative price, and one hospital is deleted because its net revenue exceeded its gross revenue. Finally, Ukiah Valley Hospital is deleted from the sample because the merger that created this hospital was being reviewed by the Federal Trade Commission through 1993. Ukiah Valley Hospital's pricing behavior may have been affected by this review.

The data for this study comes from several sources. California's Office of Statewide Health Planning and Development (OSHPAD) compiles quarterly financial data for California hospitals. PRICE, ALOS, LONGTERM, BEDSIZE, and the ownership dummy variables come from this data set.[23] OSHPAD also compiles annual data on inpatient discharges for each hospital in California. We use this data to compute CASEMIX. WAGEINDEX is simply the HCFA Medicare Wage Index for the county in which a hospital is located.[24] Finally, the data for INCOME is reported in the Summary Social, Economic, and Housing Characteristics published by the U.S. Department of Commerce. Table 1 summarizes the means and standard deviations of the variables.

IV. Results

Table 2 presents the estimated coefficients for two models in which HHI measures market power. Model 1, which constrains β_2 to equal zero, estimates a single relationship between PRICE and HHI for all hospitals. In model 1, the coefficient for HHI is positive, large, and statistically significant at the 1 percent level. This suggests that hospitals tend to set higher prices in more concentrated markets. In model 2, the variable PROFIT*HHI measures any difference between the

---

[23] OSHPAD codes Barstow Community Hospital as a for-profit hospital because it is operated by a for-profit corporation. However, the City of Barstow both owns the hospital and places some constraints on the hospital's pricing. For this reason, we have re-coded Barstow Community Hospital as a government hospital.

[24] Federal Register, Vol 60, No. 170, September 1, 1995, p. 45792.

PRICE-HHI relationship for nonprofit hospitals and for-profit hospitals. In model 2, as in model 1, the coefficient for HHI is positive, large, and statistically significant. The coefficient for PROFIT*HHI is positive and large. However, because it is not statistically significant at any standard level, we cannot reject the hypothesis that the PRICE-HHI relationship is the same for nonprofit and for-profit hospitals.

The intercept dummy variable PROFIT accounts for any difference between the intercepts for nonprofit and for-profit hospitals. The coefficient for PROFIT is large, positive, and statistically significant in model 1, where the coefficient for PROFIT*HHI is constrained to be zero. The coefficient for PROFIT is not statistically significant in model 2.

Six variables (CASEMIX, ALOS, LONGTERM, WAGEINDEX, INCOME, and BEDSIZE) measure the cost of care. The coefficient for CASEMIX is positive, large, and highly significant in both models.[25] The coefficient for ALOS, which is also positive, large, and highly significant in both models, suggests that an extra day of care costs roughly $530. The coefficient for LONGTERM is negative but not statistically significant. The coefficient for WAGEINDEX is large, positive, and highly significant in both models. In our sample, WAGEINDEX varies from 1.01 to 1.52. The estimated coefficient indicates that the price of an inpatient admission would be roughly 1400 dollars more expensive in the highest wage area than in the lowest wage area. The coefficient for INCOME is large, positive, and statistically significant, in both models. The coefficient value implies that the price of an admission rises by roughly 80 dollars for each 1000 dollar increase in the per capita income of the population that the hospital serves. Finally, the coefficient for BEDSIZE is positive and

---

[25] CASEMIX is based on the DRG weights used by the Health Care Financing Administration, which administers the Medicare program. These weights are constructed so that a diagnosis with a DRG weight of 2 should cost twice as much to treat as a diagnosis with a DRG weight of 1. If these weights accurately reflect the cost of treating diagnoses for privately insured patients, then the coefficient for CASEMIX should roughly equal the mean of PRICE divided by the mean of CASEMIX (see Table 1). It does not. Our estimate of the CASEMIX coefficient (5000 dollars) is roughly two-thirds of this quotient (6870 dollars/0.93 = 7387 dollars).

statistically significant. This suggests that larger hospitals provide a higher quality of care beyond what is accounted for by the other control variables.

Our results in Table 2 differ substantially from those of Lynk's study, which predicts that nonprofit hospitals would not exploit market power. We believe that three factors account for much of the difference between our results and Lynk's results. First, our study accounts for differences in labor costs among hospitals while his study does not. Second, our study treats district hospitals as nonprofit hospitals while his study apparently treats district hospitals as government hospitals. Third, our sample includes hospitals in Los Angeles County while his sample does not. If we re-estimate model 2 with WAGEINDEX removed as an explanatory variable, district hospitals treated as government hospitals, and hospitals in Los Angeles County deleted from our sample, then the coefficient for HHI decreases by roughly one half.

Table 3 presents the estimated regression coefficients for two models in which MINDIST1, the distance to a hospital's closest competitor, measures market power. In Model 3, which estimates a single relationship between PRICE and MINDIST1 for all hospitals by constraining β_2 to equal zero, the coefficient for MINDIST1 is positive, large, and statistically significant. The estimated coefficient suggests that a hospital can set the price per admission roughly 40 dollars higher for each additional mile of geographic differentiation that it has. In model 4, the coefficient for MINDIST1 is also positive, large, and statistically significant.[26]

In model 4, the coefficient for PROFIT*MINDIST1, which measures the difference between the PRICE-MINDIST1 relationship for nonprofit

---

[26] MINDIST1 exceeded forty miles for four observations. While the coefficient for MINDIST1 remains largely unchanged when we delete these observations, the statistical significance falls. (See Model 7 in Appendix A).

hospitals and for-profit hospitals, is negative and large, but not statistically significant. Although this result is somewhat surprising because for-profit hospitals seemingly would aggressively exploit market power, we believe that it can be largely discounted. While MINDIST1 for nonprofit hospitals ranges from 0 to 61 miles, among for-profit hospitals, the largest MINDIST1 is 19 miles and the second largest MINDIST1 is 12 miles. Thus, geographic differentiation alone gives far fewer for-profit hospitals than nonprofit hospitals the power to substantially raise price. The lack of observations in which a for-profit hospital has a large MINDIST1 may explain the above anomalous result.

Finally, the coefficient for PROFIT is positive and statistically significant at the 5 percent level in both models. As in table 2, six variables (CASEMIX, ALOS, LONGTERM, WAGEINDEX, INCOME, and BEDSIZE) control for a hospital's costs. The signs, magnitudes, and statistical significance of the coefficients for these variables are roughly the same in Table 3 as in Table 2.

V. Conclusion

In this study, we measure a hospital's market power using two alternative measures. The first is HHI computed using licensed beds in a county; the second is the distance from a hospital to its closest competitor. For both measures, we find that nonprofit hospitals set higher prices when they have more market power all else being equal. These results suggest that antitrust enforcement should challenge those mergers of nonprofit hospitals that create market power without creating offsetting efficiencies. While these results differ from Lynk's (1995) results, they are consistent with findings by Gruber (1994), Dranove et al. (1993), and Melnick et al. (1992).

Analyzing how nonprofit hospitals use whatever surplus they obtain by exploiting market power is beyond the scope of this paper. However, as noted earlier, Gruber (1994) finds that California hospitals in competitive markets decreased uncompensated care by 0.4 to 1.0 percent for each 1 percent decline in hospital resources. This suggests that at least some of the surplus that a nonprofit hospital would generate by exercising market power would be used to provide charity care. However, even if nonprofit hospitals exploit market power in part to provide charity care, society might be concerned about such an exercise of market power for two reasons. First, part of the surplus may be used for other purposes such as fancier offices. Second, from society's standpoint, an implicit tax on privately insured patients may be an inefficient means of obtaining the revenue needed to provide charity care.

References

Dranove, D., M. Stanley, and W. White, 1993, Price and concentration in hospital markets: The switch from patient-driven to payer-driven competition, Journal of Law and Economics, 36, 179-204.

Gruber, J., 1994, The effect of competitive pressure on charity: hospital responses to price shopping in California, Journal of Health Economics, 38, 183-212.

Hoerger, T., 1991, 'Profit' variability in for-profit and not-for-profit hospitals, Journal of Health Economics, 10, 259-289.

Lynk, W.J., 1994, Property rights and the presumptions of merger analysis, Antitrust Bulletin, 363-383.

Lynk, W.J., 1995, Nonprofit hospital mergers and the exercise of market power, Journal of Law and Economics, 38, 437-461.

McDonald, J.W., 1987, Competition and rail rates for the shipment of corn, soybeans, and wheat, Rand Journal of Economics, 18(1), 151-163.

Melnick, G.A., J. Zwanziger, A. Bamezai, R. Pattison, 1992, The effect of market structure and bargaining position on hospital prices, Journal of Health Economics, 11, 217-233.

Newhouse, J., 1970, Toward a theory of nonprofit institutions: An economic model of a hospital, American Economic Review, 60, 64-73.

Noether, M., 1988, Competition among hospitals, Journal of Health Economics, 7, 259-284.

Norton, E., and D. Staiger, 1994, How hospital ownership affects access to care for the uninsured, Rand Journal of Economics, 25(1), 171-185.

Pauly, M.V., and M. Redisch, 1973, The non-for-profit hospital as a physician's cooperative, American Economic Review, 63, 87-99.

Sloan, F.A., and R.A. Vraciu, 1983, Investor-owned and not-for-profit hospitals, Health Affairs, 2, 25-37.

Staten, M., J. Umbeck, and W. Dunkelberg, 1988, Market share/market power revisited: A new test for an old theory, Journal of Health Economics, 7, 73-83.

Watt, J.M., R. Derzon, S. Renn, C. Schramm, J. Hahn, and G. Pillar, 1986, The comparative economic performance of investor-owned chain and not-for-profit hospitals, New England Journal of Medicine, 314(2), 89-96.

TABLE 1

DESCRIPTIVE STATISTICS

Variables	Description	Mean	Std. Dev.	Minimum	Maximum
PRICE	average net price per discharge (private insurance)	6870	2702	1309	19671
HHI	Herfindahl-Hirschman Index for county	1822	2025	343	10000
MINDIST1	distance to a hospital's closest competitor	6.19	8.67	0.00	60.6
CASEMIX	case mix index	0.93	0.20	0.52	1.90
ALOS	average length of stay	3.97	1.15	1.99	10.20
LONGTERM	ratio of long-term days to total days	0.062	0.14	0.0	0.69
WAGEINDEX	Medicare wage index	1.21	0.14	1.01	1.52
INCOME	per capita income (county, 000's)	16.4	7.4	5.8	82.9
BEDSIZE	licensed beds	213.5	152.5	30	1094

sample:
nonprofit hospitals - 214
for-profit hospitals - 82

19

TABLE 2
REGRESSION RESULTS USING HHI

	MODEL 1	MODEL 2
INTERCEPT	-5694.04*** (1268.81)	-5692.72*** (1267.91)
HHI	0.3230*** (0.0679)	0.3054*** (0.0694)
PROFIT*HHI		0.3171 (0.2673)
CASEMIX	4811.46*** (688.07)	4715.16*** (692.36)
ALOS (average length of stay)	531.87*** (123.87)	537.10*** (123.86)
LONGTERM (long-term days/total days)	-1039.68 (872.25)	-1047.73 (871.66)
WAGEINDEX	2746.72*** (965.68)	2831.23*** (967.62)
INCOME	79.81*** (16.99)	81.47*** (17.04)
BEDSIZE	2.63*** (0.94)	2.54*** (0.94)
PROFIT	874.44*** (300.14)	554.18 (403.55)
ADJUSTED R^2	0.4482	0.4490
SAMPLE SIZE	296	296

Standard errors in parentheses
* significant at 10 percent, ** significant at 5 percent, ***
significant at 1 percent

TABLE 3
REGRESSION RESULTS USING MINDIST1

	MODEL 3	MODEL 4
INTERCEPT	-4978.74*** (1381.94)	-4906.65*** (1379.64)
MINDIST1	39.66** (16.52)	43.79*** (16.70)
PROFIT*MINDIST1		-107.92 (71.16)
CASEMIX	5065.59*** (712.35)	4999.25*** (712.09)
ALOS (average length of stay)	501.47*** (127.26)	489.97*** (127.20)
LONGTERM (long-term days/total days)	-854.06 (896.79)	-839.69 (894.82)
WAGEINDEX	2649.23** (1032.83)	2633.24** (1030.55)
INCOME	70.61*** (17.41)	70.88*** (17.37)
BEDSIZE	1.91** (0.95)	1.99** (0.94)
PROFIT	596.60** (302.41)	937.04** (376.07)
ADJUSTED R^2	0.4164	0.4190
SAMPLE SIZE	296	296

Standard errors in parentheses
* significant at 10 percent, ** significant at 5 percent, ***
significant at 1 percent

ALTERNATIVE FUNCTIONAL FORMS AND DATA SAMPLES

	Model 5	Model 6	Model 7
	log-linear (HHI)	log-linear (MINDIST1)	4 outliers (MINDIST1 >40) deleted
INTERCEPT	6.50*** (0.31)	7.53*** (0.21)	-4855*** (1409.8)
HHI	0.118*** (0.024)		
PROFIT*HHI	-0.076 (0.048)		
MINDIST1		0.047** (0.022)	39.70* (21.57)
PROFIT*MINDIST1		-0.100** (0.049)	-104.0 (72.5)
CASEMIX	0.579*** (0.105)	0.600*** (0.109)	5007*** (717)
ALOS	0.393*** (0.086)	0.353*** (0.088)	491.1*** (128.0)
LONGTERM	-0.285* (0.157)	-0.204 (0.161)	-791.6 (911.9)
WAGEINDEX	0.372*** (0.180)	0.328* (0.188)	2598** (1044)
INCOME	0.203*** (0.051)	0.187*** (0.053)	70.8*** (17.5)
BEDSIZE	0.063* (0.030)	0.035 (0.031)	1.98** (0.95)
PROFIT	0.602 (0.324)	0.146** (0.072)	919.2** (383.2)
ADJUSTED R^2	0.4098	0.3718	0.4201
SAMPLE SIZE	296	296	292

Standard errors in parentheses
* significant at 10 percent, ** significant at 5 percent, *** significant at 1 percent

PRICE-MARKET POWER REGRESSIONS FOR NONPROFIT AND DISTRICT HOSPITALS ONLY

	Model 8	Model 9
INTERCEPT	-4578.77*** (1247.34)	-4281.89*** (1362.38)
HHI	2732*** (631)	
MINDIST		40.30*** (15.16)
CASEMIX	4717.86*** (724.63)	4887.85*** (749.19)
ALOS	410.20*** (131.94)	382.82*** (135.30)
LONGTERM	-788.91 (796.11)	-683.91 (817.84)
WAGEINDEX	2729.74*** (944.00)	2979.47*** (1016.78)
INCOME	45.78** (22.39)	32.05 (22.77)
BEDSIZE	3.11*** (0.90)	2.52*** (0.90)
ADJUSTED R^2	0.4473	0.4170
SAMPLE SIZE	214	214

standard errors in parentheses
* significant at 10 percent, ** significant at 5 percent, *** significant at 1 percent

www.ingramcontent.com/pod-product-compliance
Lightning Source LLC
Chambersburg PA
CBHW081250170526
45165CB00009B/3276